OUT OF THE LAB
EXTREME JOBS IN SCIENCE

VOLCANOLOGISTS AND SEISMOLOGISTS

by Ruth Owen

PowerKiDS press

New York

Published in 2014 by The Rosen Publishing Group, Inc.
29 East 21st Street, New York, NY 10010

First Edition

Produced for Rosen by Ruby Tuesday Books Ltd
Editor for Ruby Tuesday Books Ltd: Mark J. Sachner
US Editor: Joshua Shadowens
Designer: Emma Randall

Photo Credits:
Cover, 1, 4, 5, 8–9, 12, 19, 26–27, 29 © Shutterstock; 5 (top) © Ruby Tuesday Books; 6–7 © Superstock; 10–11, 13, 24 © Science Photo Library; 15 © Public Domain; 17, 18, 23, 25 © USGS; 20–21 © Wikipedia Creative Commons.

Publisher Cataloging Data

Owen, Ruth.
Volcanologists and seismologists / by Ruth Owen. — First edition.
  p. cm. — (Out of the lab: extreme jobs in science)
Includes index.
ISBN 978-1-4777-1292-4 (library binding) — ISBN 978-1-4777-1382-2 (pbk.) — ISBN 978-1-4777-1383-9 (6-pack)
1. Seismologists — Juvenile literature. 2. Volcanologists — Juvenile literature. 3. Seismology — Juvenile literature. 4. Volcanology — Juvenile literature. I. Owen, Ruth, 1967–. II. Title.
QE521.3 O94 2014
551.21—dc23

Manufactured in the United States of America

CPSIA Compliance Information: Batch #S13PK8: For Further Information contact Rosen Publishing, New York, New York at 1-800-237-9932

Contents

RESTLESS PLANET

You may have seen TV news reports about a **volcano** erupting or a devastating **earthquake**. But what causes these violent natural **phenomena**?

Earth's rocky outer crust is broken into large pieces called **tectonic plates.** The plates are constantly moving against each other, squeezing and stretching the rocks that make up the crust. This creates the underground conditions that cause earthquakes to occur.

Below the Earth's crust is the mantle. Here, it is so hot that rock melts and forms thick, oozing, **molten** rock called **magma.** Sometimes when the Earth's crust moves and cracks, it allows an opening in the crust to appear through which magma can escape. Over time, a mountain, called a volcano, forms above this opening.

SCIENCE IN ACTION

Earth is made up of three layers called the crust, the mantle, and the core. The crust ranges in thickness from just 3 miles (4.8 km) to 35 miles (56 km).

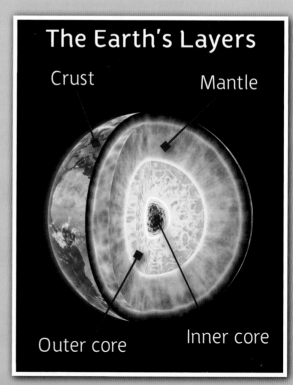

The Earth's Layers

Crust

Mantle

Outer core

Inner core

The red lines on this map show the edges of Earth's tectonic plates. The plates fit together like a giant jigsaw puzzle.

A volcano erupting

THE SCIENCE OF OUR PLANET

The scientific study of Earth and how it works is called **geology**.

Geologists are scientists who study how Earth formed and what it is made of. They study the planet's rocky surface, its internal structure, and naturally occurring phenomena such as earthquakes. There are many different branches of geology. The branch of geology that deals with the science of volcanoes is called **volcanology**. **Seismology** is the study of earthquakes.

SCIENCE IN ACTION

While a lot of work takes place in a **laboratory** or at a computer in an office, a volcanologist or seismologist gets plenty of chances to work outside doing **fieldwork**. This work often takes place in extreme environments, such as on the tops of mountains!

It will never be possible to stop volcanoes erupting or earthquakes happening. Many scientists choose to become **volcanologists** or **seismologists**, however, because they want to help find ways to predict when one of these disasters might take place. Any advance warning of an earthquake or volcanic eruption could save many lives.

Two volcanologists collecting gas samples from a volcano

HOW A VOLCANO WORKS

When a volcanologist is working in the field, his or her workplace is a volcano. And workplaces don't come much more extreme than that!

A volcano is a self-made mountain that starts life as a hole in the Earth's crust. This hole is called a vent. Beneath the crust is the mantle, which is made up of rocks and magma. During a volcanic eruption, gases beneath the crust force magma out of the vent and onto the Earth's surface. The magma pours or blasts from the vent covering the surrounding ground. Once the magma is on the surface, it cools and hardens to form new rock. Each time a volcano erupts, a new layer of rock is added to the land around the vent until eventually a mountain forms. On the mountaintop is a large opening called a **crater**.

This simple diagram shows the structure of a volcano.

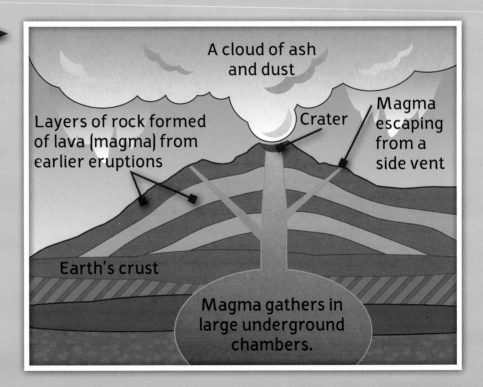

A cloud of ash and dust

Layers of rock formed of lava (magma) from earlier eruptions

Crater

Magma escaping from a side vent

Earth's crust

Magma gathers in large underground chambers.

Magma erupting from Mount Stromboli's crater

Mount Stromboli is a volcano on one of Sicily's islands

SCIENCE IN ACTION

Once magma has reached Earth's surface, it is known as **lava**. This oozing, superhot material can sometimes be hot enough to melt the rocks it touches on the surface!

LIFE AS A VOLCANOLOGIST

All volcanologists will tell you their work is very exciting, and once they start studying volcanoes, they don't want to stop!

Volcanologists study active volcanoes, extinct, or dead, volcanoes, and dormant volcanoes. A dormant volcano is one that has not erupted in a very long time. There are about 600 active volcanoes in the world today, so volcanologists get the chance to travel far and wide to carry out their investigations.

Volcanologists study volcanoes to understand how and why they erupt, how eruptions can be predicted, and how the activities of volcanoes affect the environment and living things, including humans. Many volcanologists work for government agencies monitoring their country's volcanoes so that people can be warned if an eruption is going to happen.

A volcanologist films lava flow on the slopes of Mount Etna, a volcano in Sicily. He is wearing a gas mask to avoid breathing in poisonous gases.

SCIENCE IN ACTION

A volcanologist may work at a volcano observatory, which is a research center built close to a volcano. At the observatory, scientists study and keep track of all the volcano's activities.

ALL IN A DAY'S WORK

When carrying out fieldwork, volcanologists may have to hike for miles (km) or climb mountains to reach the place they want to study. Fieldwork may also mean living in a tent for days or weeks at a time.

A typical day's work on a research trip will involve making observations, drawing sketches, writing notes, taking photographs, and collecting samples of rock, lava, and gases.

A volcanologist's work gear usually includes hiking boots, jeans, and a jacket, or overalls. If working on slopes with lots of loose rocks or on a volcano where rocks may be blasted from the crater, a rock-climbing helmet is essential. Volcanologists also carry gas masks because volcanoes may emit poisonous gases.

 Mount Erebus is a volcano in Antarctica, the coldest place on Earth! Volcanologists often climb to the top of this mountain to study its volcanic activities.

A volcanologist
wearing a
heat-resistant,
protective suit

Very occasionally, a
volcanologist might need to
wear a silver, heat-resistant
suit when carrying out
investigations on a volcano.
These suits are very bulky,
however, and make it difficult
to move around and work.

GETTING UP CLOSE WITH LAVA

One of the field tasks carried out by volcanologists is collecting samples of lava.

Samples are collected from lava flows that are slowly oozing from cracks in the volcano's slopes. Wearing thick, protective gloves a volcanologist uses a hammer to part chop and part scoop a sample of lava from the flow. The lava looks like glowing, melted toffee. It's very dangerous stuff, however, because the temperature of lava can reach 2,000°F (1,110°C).

The sample, or blob, of lava is dropped into cold water inside a metal container. It quickly cools and hardens and can then be taken back to the laboratory to be studied.

A volcanologist collecting a ▶ lava sample using a hammer

By analyzing the chemical make-up of a sample of lava, scientists can find out about the processes happening inside the volcano and even in the mantle far below.

Lava flow

COLLECTING DATA

The rock on the slopes of a volcano may sometimes slide, bulge outwards, or move in other ways.

These movements can sometimes be a sign that there is activity happening inside the volcano and it is building up to an eruption.

Volcanologists monitor movements on a volcano using **GPS (Global Positioning System)** equipment. They fix steel bolts into rock on the volcano's slopes. Then they set up a GPS sensor above each bolt. The sensors precisely pinpoint the bolts' positions. If the rock then moves, the sensors will record the bolts' new positions and show the scientists that movements have occurred.

SCIENCE IN ACTION

The movements of a volcano's rock might only be a few inches (cm) over several months. This would be difficult for a person to accurately notice with their eyes. The GPS data, however, will show the scientists if even the tiniest movements have happened.

A scientist with a GPS sensor on Mount St. Helens, in Washington State. Mount Adams volcano can be seen in the distance.

MEET A VOLCANOLOGIST

Richard Herd is a British volcanologist who has spent time working at the Montserrat Volcano Observatory, in the Caribbean.

Richard says that working with volcanoes has the potential to be dangerous, but like all volcanologists he doesn't take risks. When working on a very active volcano, you fly to the volcano's crater or slopes by helicopter, carry out your investigations quickly, then fly out again. It can be unnerving, however, working on the slopes of a volcano. Richard recalls hearing the crash of rocks falling down the volcano's slopes and feeling the ground shaking as earthquakes happen underground.

Volcanologists often fly over volcanoes in helicopters to see how they are growing and changing.

When a field trip is complete, it's back to the office or laboratory to analyze the samples and data. A volcanologist will have reports to write and will sometimes use computer programs to create predictions of how a volcano might act in the future based on the data that's been collected.

Montserrat's Soufrière Hills volcano erupting in 1995

INTO THE VOLCANO

In October 2010, Icelandic volcanologist Dr. Freysteinn Sigmundsson and his team mounted the first ever expedition into a volcano.

The Thrihnukagigur volcano in Iceland is dormant, or sleeping, and last erupted 3,000 years ago. It could come back to life at any time, though.

The team descended below ground level into what was once the volcano's magma chamber. The magma chamber is the area below a volcano where the magma collects. Scientists have previously climbed into the craters of dormant volcanoes, but no one has ever explored a volcano's deepest depths. The expedition will help scientists learn more about the insides of volcanoes and how they work.

This is a view from inside Thrihnukagigur. One scientist said, "Thrihnukagigur is unique. It's like somebody came and pulled the plug and all the magma ran down out of it."

SCIENCE IN ACTION

The team that explored Thrihnukagigur included scientists, expert mountain climbers, a photographer, and a film crew. The team used ropes to lower themselves the 650 feet (198 m) down into the magma chamber.

HOW AN EARTHQUAKE HAPPENS

Earth's tectonic plates are constantly sliding past each other and it is this movement that causes earthquakes.

Sometimes, the rough edges of two plates will get jammed. The plates keep moving, however, causing a massive amount of energy and pressure to build up deep underground at the point where the plate edges are stuck together.

Finally, the continued movement of the plates causes the jammed edges to come unstuck and the two plates suddenly slip past each other. In that instant, all the stored-up energy and pressure is released into the ground and an earthquake happens. The energy radiates outward in all directions in waves. The waves shake the Earth and when they reach the surface, the shaking causes buildings to collapse and other terrible damage.

The devastation caused by a powerful earthquake that happened in Chile in February, 2010.

The waves created by an earthquake are called **seismic waves**. They radiate out from the hypocenter (the point where the earthquake happened underground) like ripples on a pond.

EARTHQUAKE SCIENTIST

Seismologists are the scientists who study earthquakes.

An earthquake may happen miles (km) underground, so to find out how powerful the earthquake was a seismologist uses an instrument called a seismograph to record seismic waves. The recording made by a seismograph is called a seismogram. It can be shown digitally or on paper, and it looks like a jagged line. The longer and more jagged the line, the more powerful the earthquake.

The work of seismologists helps us to understand more about how earthquakes work. By measuring seismic activity in the ground, scientists can warn that an area may be at risk of earthquakes in the future. As yet, however, scientists have not developed a way to predict exactly when an earthquake will happen in a particular area.

A seismogram recording of a powerful earthquake that occurred in Afghanistan in 2002

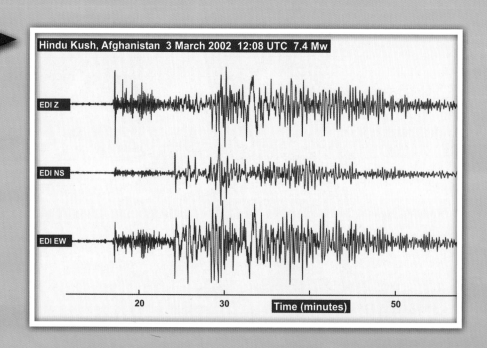

Being a seismologist can be a physically demanding job. These scientists may spend time outside in all types of weather, working day or night to collect and record data. They may also have to hike long distances in remote places to gather their research.

Doug Given (left) is a US seismologist. Following the 2010 earthquake in Haiti, Doug traveled to the country to set up seismographs and do research in the area.

SEISMOLOGY IN ACTION

In January 2010, a catastrophic earthquake hit Haiti. French seismologist Eric Calais has been helping Haiti rebuild and prepare for the future.

By studying the ground in Haiti, Eric has been able to advise where the best places to rebuild will be. Some types of ground withstand seismic waves better than others, so rebuilding homes on stronger ground is important.

SCIENCE IN ACTION

Like volcanologists, when a disaster occurs, a seismologist may need to travel to a disaster zone on the other side of the world to help investigate what has happened.

New buildings should also be constructed in ways that can better withstand earthquakes. Eric also advised that Haiti should have a system in place to monitor seismic activity and give warnings of possible future earthquakes.

Scientific data shows that some time in the future Haiti will suffer an even bigger earthquake than the one in 2010. Eric's work is helping the people of Haiti to prepare for this threat.

Before the earthquake struck Haiti in 2010, this rubble-strewn area was a building in the capital city of Port au Prince.

PART SCIENTIST, PART ADVENTURER

A career as a seismologist or volcanologist working in the field will definitely be extreme!

You might travel to an area that has just experienced an earthquake and be working there when further earthquakes or **aftershocks** occur. Studying a volcano that is about to erupt might mean a sudden evacuation by helicopter to escape scorching lava, explosions, or poisonous clouds of gas. Science is not a Hollywood movie, though.

No matter how extreme the conditions you are working in, you must carry out your scientific research with extreme care and precision. You must also be ready for the long, unglamorous hours of painstaking analysis back at the lab. If you're looking for a career that's part science and part adventure, however, seismology or volcanology could be for you!

A massive ash cloud erupts from a ➤ volcano as a volcanologist watches.

When asked to describe his job, one volcanologist said, "Working with volcanoes appeals to the kid in you— the excitement, the danger, the thrill of watching things blow up. I get to look at some really cool things."

GLOSSARY

aftershocks (AF-ter-shoks)
Small earthquakes that follow a larger, main earthquake.

crater (KRAY-tur)
A circular depression that forms the mouth of a volcano.

earthquake (URTH-kwayk)
A naturally occurring phenomenon caused by Earth's tectonic plates making a sudden movement that sends out waves of energy through the ground, which cause severe shaking on the surface.

fieldwork (FEELD-wurk) Scientific work that takes place outside instead of in a laboratory.

geology (jee-AH-luh-jee)
The scientific study of Earth, including its formation and structure, surface features such as volcanoes, and naturally occurring phenomena such as earthquakes.

GPS (Global Positioning System) (GLOH-bul puh-ZIH-shun-ing SIS-tum) A device that helps find your location on a map.

laboratory (LA-bruh-tor-ee)
A room, building, and sometimes a vehicle where there is equipment that can be used to carry out experiments and other scientific studies.

lava (LAH-vuh)
Hot liquid rock that has erupted or poured from a volcano. When this material is still inside the volcano, it is known as magma.

magma (MAG-muh)
Underground rock that has become so hot it melts.

molten (MOHL-ten)
Melted, or liquefied, by heat.

phenomena (FEE-noh-meh-nah)
Unusual events that one can see or feel.

seismic waves (SYZ-mik WAYVZ) Waves of energy that radiate through the ground following an earthquake.

seismologists (syz-MAH-luh-jists) Scientists who study seismic waves and earthquakes.

seismology (syz-MAH-luh-jee) The scientific study of earthquakes and seismic waves. Seismology is a branch of geology.

tectonic plates (tek-TAH-nik PLAYTS) The huge pieces of the Earth's crust that fit together like the pieces of a jigsaw.

volcano (vol-KAY-noh) An opening in the Earth's surface, often formed on a hill or a mountain, from which lava can erupt.

volcanologists (vol-kuh-NAH-luh-jists) Scientists who study volcanoes.

volcanology (vol-kuh-NAH-luh-jee) The scientific study of volcanoes. Volcanology is a branch of geology.

WEBSITES

Due to the changing nature of Internet links, PowerKids Press has developed an online list of websites related to the subject of this book. This site is updated regularly. Please use this link to access the list:

www.powerkidslinks.com/olejs/volcan/

READ MORE

Green, Jen. *Understanding Volcanoes and Earthquakes*. Our Earth. New York: PowerKids Press, 2008.

Prokos, Anna. *Earthquakes*. The Ultimate 10: Natural Disasters. New York: Gareth Stevens Hi-Lo Must Read!, 2008.

Spilsbury, Louise, and Richard Spilsbury. *Violent Volcanoes*. Awesome Forces of Nature. Mankato, MN: Heinemann, 2011.

INDEX